Planets, Moons and Meteors

Meteors

THE YOUNG STARGAZER'S GUIDE TO THE GALAXY

By John Gustafson

JULIAN Ⓜ MESSNER

Library of Congress Cataloging-in-Publication Data

Gustafson, John R.
    Planets, moons and meteors / by John R. Gustafson.
        p.   cm. — (The young stargazer's guide to the galaxy)
    Includes index.
    Summary: Describes planets, moons, meteors, and other objects
in the solar system and how to find them with the naked eye,
binoculars, or a telescope.
    1. Astronomy— Observers' manuals—Juvenile literature.
[1. Astronomy— Observers' manuals.] I. Title. II. Title: Planets,
moons, and meteors. III. Series.
QB63.G87 1992
523—dc20   91-25908
ISBN 0-671-72534-3 (LSB)   CIP
ISBN 0-671-72535-1 (pbk.)   AC

Published by Julian Messner, a division of Simon & Schuster,
Simon & Schuster Building, Rockefeller Center, 1230 Avenue of the
Americas, New York, NY 10020.

Produced by: RGA Publishing Group, Inc.
Project Editor: Lisa Melton
Design: Heidi Frieder and Hi-Rez Studio
Cover design: Virginia Pope-Boehling
Illustrations: Mark Brest van Kempen
Photo credits on page 63

Manufactured in the United States of America
10   9   8   7   6   5   4   3   2   1

To Elena and Nathaniel

**Special thanks to John Hodge
for proposing the book
and sticking with it.**

523
GUS

CONTENTS

Sun

Mercury   Earth

Venus   Mars

Jupiter   Saturn   Uranus   Neptune   Pluto

The Solar System, showing the relative sizes of each planet as compared to the Sun. From the left: the Sun, Mercury, Venus, Earth, Mars, Jupiter, Saturn, Uranus, Neptune, Pluto.

OUR BIG BACKYARD: THE SOLAR SYSTEM

1

The Earth is so big that you can't possibly get to know every place or person on it. You can, however, become very familiar with the area near where you live, because you spend so much time there. You get to know your neighbors, the houses on your street, and especially your own backyard or neighborhood park.

The **universe**, of course, is an even bigger place than the Earth. It is filled with countless galaxies, each containing billions of stars. Although astronomers spend years studying the universe, even they can't become familiar with everything in it. But any of us can get to know the part of the universe in which we live—the **Solar System**—which is like our big backyard.

It is possible to get to know many parts of the Solar System using only your eyes. And if you use a pair of binoculars or a small telescope, you'll find that other parts of the Solar System also come into view.

The term "Solar System" comes from the word *sol*, which is the Latin word for "Sun." The Sun stands at the center of the Solar System. Its gravity keeps all the other bodies—planets, moons, meteors, and more—orbiting around it.

Like steam rising from boiling water, a cloud of invisible particles rises from the Sun's surface and blows through the Solar System at about 700,000 miles per hour. Far beyond the last planet, the **solar wind** slows down and is finally overwhelmed by winds from other stars. Some say that this point in space should be considered the outermost limit of the Solar System. Nobody knows how far away the boundary is, but the Voyager and Pioneer spacecraft are measuring the solar wind as they travel to the edge of the Solar System. In the next decade or two, one of these spacecraft may reach that boundary and tell us just how big our Solar System is.

Nine **planets** orbit around the Sun: **Mercury, Venus, Earth, Mars, Jupiter, Saturn, Uranus, Neptune**, and **Pluto**. Most of the planets are themselves orbited by natural bodies called **satellites**. (Natural satellites are sometimes called moons; Earth's satellite is always called the **Moon**.)

In addition to planets and satellites, the Solar System contains many thousands of **asteroids**, which are chunks of rock and metal circling the Sun in their own orbits. Most of the asteroids fall within the **Asteroid Belt**, an area between the orbits of Mars and Jupiter. The smallest ones we can see from Earth are about the size of small hills and the biggest are about the size of Texas.

The Solar System also is filled with countless **meteoroids**. Most of these pieces of rock and metal are no bigger than a grain of sand, but some can be as big as a house. Large meteoroids were plentiful when

TRY THIS . . .

MAKING A SCALE MODEL OF THE SOLAR SYSTEM

You can use common objects to show the relative sizes of the Sun and planets.

Grab a basketball and let that represent the Sun. A quarter can represent Jupiter, the biggest planet, and a nickel can stand for Saturn, the second-biggest planet. Two unpopped kernels of popcorn can represent Uranus and Neptune. Take two seeds from a cherry tomato for Venus and Earth, two poppy seeds for Mercury and Mars, and a grain of salt for Pluto—and you've got the makings of your own Solar System!

Now think about how far apart you would have to place your substitute planets to create an accurate scale model of the solar system. Picture in your mind a baseball diamond. If you were to put the basketball representing the Sun at home plate, you would put a poppy seed for Mercury, the closest planet, about halfway to the pitcher's mound. The tomato seed for Venus would be just in front of the pitcher's mound. Earth's tomato seed would be about midway between the pitcher's mound and second base. Mars, another poppy seed, would be in the outfield, just beyond second base. Jupiter, the quarter, would be beyond the centerfield fence, even in the biggest major league ballpark. The nickel representing Saturn would be outside the ballpark. And Pluto, the tiny grain of salt, would be more than half a mile away from home plate!

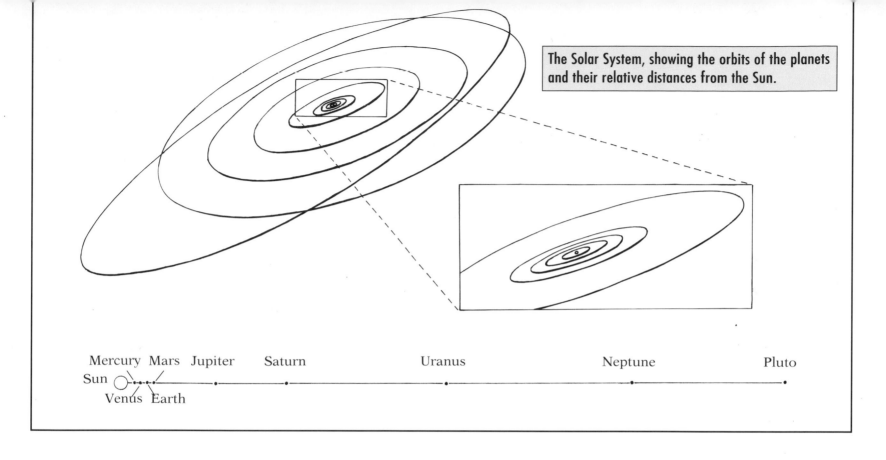

The Solar System, showing the orbits of the planets and their relative distances from the Sun.

Mercury Mars Jupiter Saturn Uranus Neptune Pluto
Sun
Venus Earth

the Solar System was young, but now they are very rare. When a meteoroid enters Earth's atmosphere, it burns up, creating a bright streak we call a **meteor**, or shooting star. If a meteoroid does not burn up completely in the atmosphere but instead lands on Earth, we call it a **meteorite**. Some of these are no bigger than pieces of dust and are called **micrometeorites**.

Finally, the Solar System contains millions of **comets**, each orbiting the Sun. These are lumps of frozen gas and water mixed with rocky particles. Most of these particles are as small as dust. The comets we observe usually have long, cigar-shaped orbits that take them far beyond Pluto. We see one only when its orbit changes and it comes close to the Sun. Then, the Sun's energy boils off the ice and

The Sun is the center of our Solar System. This photo shows the Sun's chromosphere, which is made mostly of hydrogen gas. Because of a special camera filter, the prominences look like dark spots against the Sun (a discussion of prominences appears on page 29). The Sun is so large that if you put together all the planets, moons, comets, and other bodies in the Solar System, the Sun would still be 500 times bigger.

Mercury

Venus

Earth

Mars

Jupiter

Saturn

Uranus

Neptune

Pluto

9

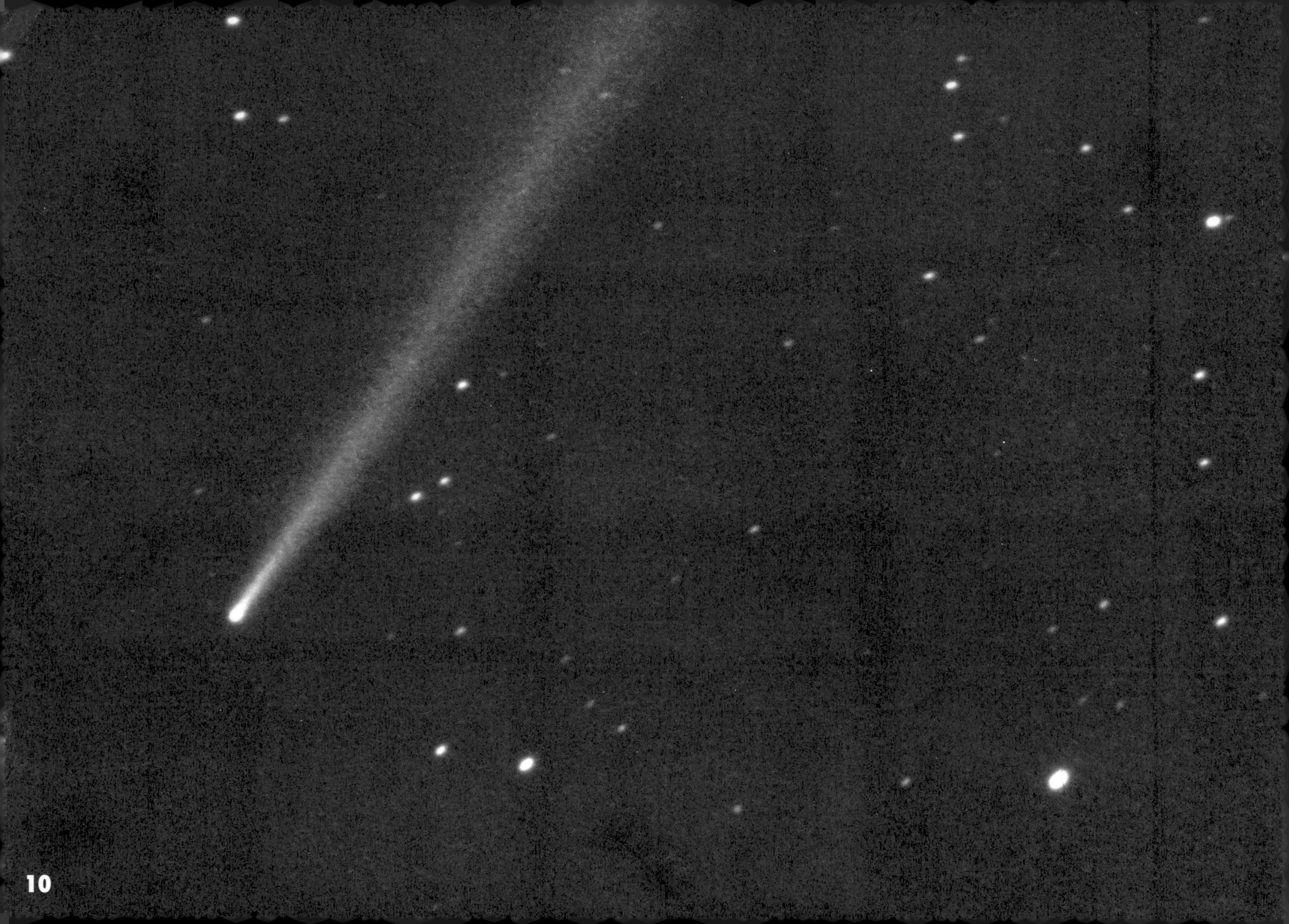

10

frozen gases in the comet, causing it to give off a huge glowing gas cloud bright enough for us to see.

If you were to clump together all the Solar System's planets, moons, asteroids, meteoroids, and comets—everything except the Sun—do you suppose this clump would be as big as the Sun? It would not even be close! In fact, the clump would have to be 500 times bigger just to match the size of the Sun. The Sun contains 99.8 percent of all the material in the Solar System. The planets and all the other objects in the Solar System are "debris" left over from the time it formed. Fortunately for us, one of those pieces of debris is a fairly nice place we call Earth. The Earth is not so close to the Sun that it is too hot, like Mercury, or so far away from the Sun that it is completely frozen, like Pluto. Earth also is about the right size for retaining an atmosphere of the kind needed to support life as we know it. You might say that Earth is like the third bowl of porridge in the story of Goldilocks: it's not too hot, and it's not too cold. It's the perfect size, too. In fact, it's just right!

LEFT: One of the brightest comets ever seen, comet Ikeya-Seki was discovered by and named after two Japanese amateur astronomers, who captured this amazing sight on film with a 35-mm camera on November 2, 1965. RIGHT: The Leonid meteor shower of 1966 poured down countless meteors over the western United States. Meteors are the bright streaks of light made when a meteoroid enters the Earth's atmosphere. There are more than 100 meteors falling in this photograph!

This rare shot of the Moon and four planets situated together was taken on the morning of August 14, 1966. To the right of the large Moon is Mars, then Jupiter. Below the Moon is Venus, then faint Mercury just above the trees.

TIPS FOR STARGAZERS

2

BASICS OF OBSERVATION

Observing the sky is as easy as stepping outside on a clear night and using your eyes. It also takes patience: not everything in the Solar System can be seen on any single night. To see all the different phases of the Moon, for example, you have to watch as it changes over a month's time. And you'll have to wait until the year 2061 to see Halley's comet!

When you look at the night sky, one of the first things you will notice is that some stars seem to be grouped in patterns. Skywatchers in ancient times played "connect the dots" with these stars and gave the resulting shapes special names. These groups of stars are called **constellations**. People named the constellations after animals or other familiar objects—whatever they thought the shapes looked like. This helped them to remember the many stars in the sky. Modern stargazers still use constellations to help find their way around the night sky.

The stars in a constellation often are not actually close together in space. Some are nearby and others are much farther away. But they all lie in the same general direction, so from our perspective here on Earth they appear to be close to one another in the sky.

One of the easiest constellations to find is the Big Dipper, which has seven stars that form the outline of a ladle with a curved handle. The Big Dipper is visible throughout the year from the Northern Hemisphere, the area on Earth north of the equator. It is actually part of a larger constellation called Ursa Major, which means "big bear."

To find your way around the sky, it helps to know directions. The Earth's main directions—north, south, east, and west—are defined by the planet's spin. If you imagine Earth as a figure skater spinning on the ice, her head would be the North Pole and her feet would be the South Pole. Her arms swinging around from her sides would be positioned like the Earth's equator, moving west to east. Because the Earth spins, it defines these directions for us naturally.

If you keep thinking of the Earth as a spinning ice skater, then you can imagine that the stars in the sky are like the audience in the stands of the skating rink. The audience sees the skater spinning around,

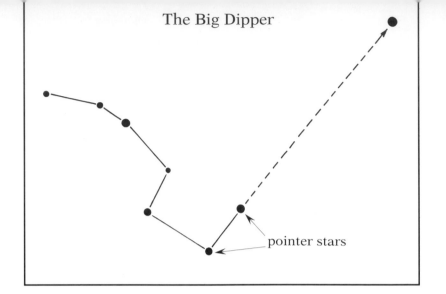

The Big Dipper

pointer stars

TRY THIS . . .

FINDING DIRECTIONS ON EARTH

It's easy to find which way is north. Choose a sunny, bright day. Go outside at noon (or 1:00 P.M. during daylight time) and stand so the Sun is at your back. Your shadow will then point to the north (for those of us in the Northern Hemisphere).

But how do you find which way is north at night, when you don't have the Sun to help you? You look for Polaris, which is also called the North Star. If you can find the Big Dipper, you can find Polaris. If you draw a line

between the two stars at the front edge of the Big Dipper it would point toward the North Star. These two stars in the Big Dipper are called "pointer stars" because they point the way.

Once you have found north, you can locate the directions of east and west. Lie on your back with your head toward the north. Stick out your left arm to the side and it points to the east. Your right arm sticking out to the side points to the west. Now raise your left arm and sweep it toward your right side. Imagine the stars rising in the east and moving in the direction of your arm's motion, toward the west. It takes the stars about 12 hours to make the journey.

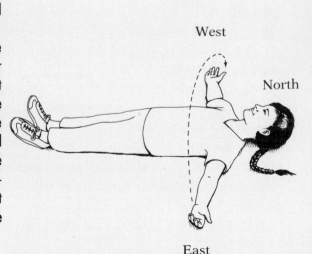

West

North

East

just as we would see the Earth spinning around if we looked at it from distant space. But the skater could pretend that she is holding still and the audience is revolving around her. That's what it's like to us here on Earth: it seems as though we are holding still and the sky is moving around us. The Sun, Moon, and stars appear to rise in the east, cross overhead, and set in the west.

Our ancestors studied the sky for hundreds of years before they understood that the sky holds still and the Earth itself spins. We still say that the Sun, moon, planets and stars rise and set, even though we now know that it's our Earth which is moving.

Once you have learned directions, you need to be able to measure distances in the sky. Astronomers use **angular distances** to make sky measurements. Angular distances are measured in **degrees**, based on the 360 degrees contained in a circle. If you face north and then turn around to face south you have turned through 180 degrees. Ninety degrees away from the **horizon** (the line where the Earth meets the sky) is the **zenith** (the point directly overhead). You can learn to estimate smaller angular distances by using your hand as a "ruler."

TRY THIS . . .

MEASURING DISTANCES IN THE SKY

The width of the Moon as seen in the sky is one-half a degree. The width of a finger held at arm's length is about one degree. Do you think your finger can cover the Moon?

When the Moon is up, stretch out your arm and hold up one finger. Close one eye and compare the width of your finger to the size of the Moon. (You may find it easier to try this measurement during the day or at twilight, when the Moon does not seem so bright.) Your finger should appear about twice as big as the Moon. You now have your first "ruler" for measuring distances between stars.

Your fist held at arm's length spans about 10 degrees. Compare your fist to the width of the bowl in the Big Dipper. They should look about the same size (remember to close one eye). Can you find another set of stars that looks about 10 degrees wide?

If you hold your hand at arm's length and spread your fingers out as wide as you can, there will be about 20 degrees from the tip of your little finger to the tip of your thumb. The North Star is about 30 degrees from the two pointer stars in the Big Dipper. Can you measure this distance, using your fist and outstretched hand in combination?

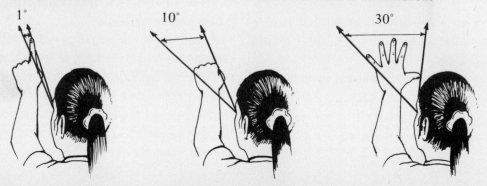

Once you know how to recognize certain constellations, find directions, and measure distances in the sky, you will be able to find objects in the sky with the help of a **star chart**. Star charts show the locations of the major constellations and most of the bright stars in the sky. Astronomers use star charts in much the same way that travelers use road maps. While road maps use miles or kilometers to show distances between towns, star charts use degrees to show distances between stars. With a little practice, you will be able to use a star chart as easily as you can use a road map. A typical star chart is included at right to help you get started.

One convenient type of star chart is called a **planisphere**. A planisphere shows the entire sky as seen from a particular place or latitude. It can be adjusted to show the sky as seen from that place any hour of the night, any night of the year.

Another important tool astronomers use is an **observation log**. In these logs, astronomers write the name of each object they study, the date, the weather conditions, and where they were when they made the observations, along with any special conditions they might have noted. You can keep your own observation log in a notebook.

NAKED-EYE OBSERVATION

Before telescopes were invented, people had only their eyes to use in studying the sky. This is called naked-eye observation. You can see many things in the sky

TRY THIS . . .

USING STAR CHARTS

Practice using star charts to locate some constellations in the night sky. The star chart on page 17 shows how the sky looks during spring. The top of the star chart is north, but notice that the directions east and west are reversed from the way they look on maps of, say, the town in which you live. How did this happen?

Consider if you were lying on your stomach with your head pointing north. In front of you on the ground lies a road map. On the map, east is to the right, just as your right arm is to the east, and west is left.

But what happens if you roll over on your back, keeping your head to the north, so you are looking up at the sky? Suddenly east is to your left and west is to your right. This is the orientation astronomers use for their star charts. Astronomers are used to "thinking backwards" when they read star charts, and with a little practice you will be, too.

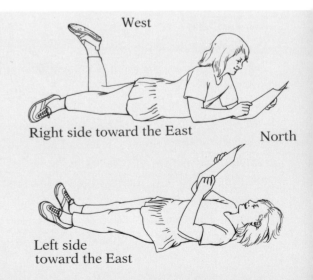

West

Right side toward the East

North

Left side toward the East

using only your eyes. This is still the best way to begin your adventures in astronomy and learn your way around the sky. In fact, meteors are easier to spot with the naked eye than with a telescope because your eye can scan much more of the sky at once than can a telescope.

For your stargazing, find a place that's fairly dark. Many people live in cities or towns where

streetlights and buildings cast light into the sky. Make sure you're not directly under a streetlight. In fact, the farther away from a light you are, the better. In a dark spot away from a city or town you can see hundreds of stars twinkling in the night sky.

Once you are in a dark spot, it will take your eyes about 10 minutes to adjust fully to the darkness. As your eyes adjust and become more sensitive, many faint stars will come into view. You'll want to bring along a flashlight for looking at your star charts and for writing in your observation log, but it's important to keep your eyes adjusted to the dark. Since our eyes are not as sensitive to red light as to other colors, you can use a red flashlight to read your charts and your eyes will still remain adjusted to the dark. To make your flashlight "astronomy safe," use tape or a rubber band to attach red cellophane or plastic to the front. (Note: Having a chair or cushion that lets you lean back comfortably will make observing more pleasant. If you stand and look up for very long, your neck will become stiff and you will tire quickly.)

BINOCULAR AND TELESCOPE OBSERVATION

A pair of binoculars or a small telescope can bring many objects into view. The openings on telescopes and binoculars are much bigger than the pupils of your eyes, so they can collect more light than your

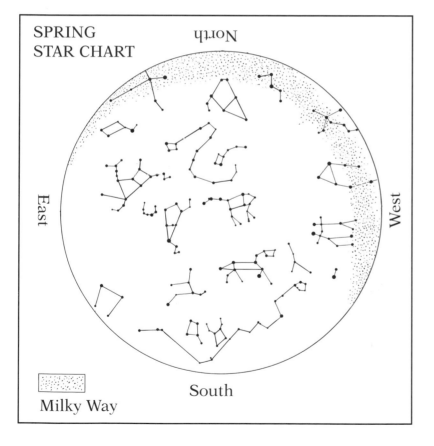

SPRING STAR CHART

North

East

West

South

Milky Way

eyes can. The light is then **focused** into an image you can see. Some telescopes, called refractors, use lenses to focus light (binoculars do, too). Other telescopes, called reflectors, use mirrors to focus the light.

Refractors were the first type of telescope invented. Light passing through a piece of glass changes direction, or is "refracted." If a glass lens is curved just right, the light will bend to form a concentrated, focused image. A simple refractor has a large lens called the objective lens and a smaller lens called the eyepiece. The two lenses work in combination to create an image that's the right size to enter your pupil. A reflector also uses a small lens for the eyepiece, but instead of a large lens for the objective, it uses a curved mirror, which bends and concentrates light just as the lens in a refractor does.

In addition to focusing light into a bright image, telescopes and binoculars also magnify, or enlarge, objects or make them look larger or closer. For example, to the naked eye a planet such as Jupiter appears to be simply a point of light—no different from a bright star in the sky. But through a telescope or binoculars you can see that Jupiter is a disk, not just a point. Craters on the Moon also become much more dramatic when viewed through a pair of binoculars or a telescope.

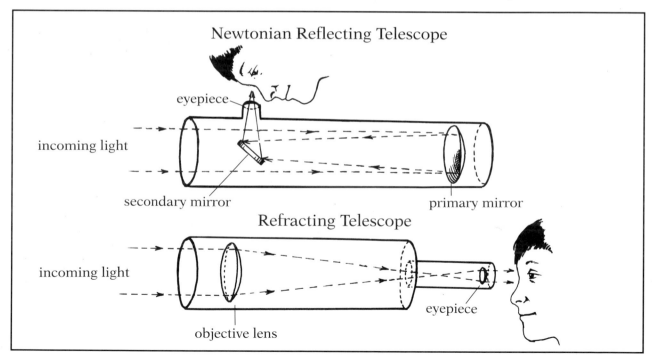

Newtonian Reflecting Telescope

eyepiece

incoming light

secondary mirror

primary mirror

Refracting Telescope

incoming light

eyepiece

objective lens

TRY THIS . . .

LEARNING HOW A TELESCOPE WORKS

You can demonstrate how a refractor telescope works with some simple hand lenses, which you can get at a local hobby store or through a mail-order company. Ask for two double convex lenses with different focal lengths: one about 10 to 14 inches, the other about 1 to 2 inches.

You can measure the focal lengths of your lenses at home. Stand near an inside wall opposite a brightly lit window. Hold one of the lenses near the wall (don't block the window with your body). Move the lens toward or away from the wall until you form an image of the window on the wall. When the window's image is in focus, the distance between the lens and the wall is the focal length of the lens. Measure the focal length of both lenses.

Notice that the size of the window's image is different for the two lenses. The lens with the longer focal length makes a larger image. You'll also see that the window's image is upside down. Lenses turn things upside down, and you have to get used to this when using some telescopes. (Binoculars include prism-shaped mirrors that turn the images right-side up again.)

With your two lenses you can now see how a telescope works. Let the lens with the longer focal length be the objective; the other lens is your eyepiece. Add the focal lengths of the two lenses together. The sum is the length of your telescope. Hold the two lenses apart at about this distance (the sum of the focal lengths). Now look through your eyepiece at your objective. When you get the spacing between the two lenses just right, you will be able to bring distant objects into focus. You have just made a telescope!

Notice that there is a very specific point at which an image comes into focus. Once you have the image in focus, try tilting the eyepiece. Does the image become distorted? The lenses in a telescope have to be very carefully aligned to get clear, sharp images.

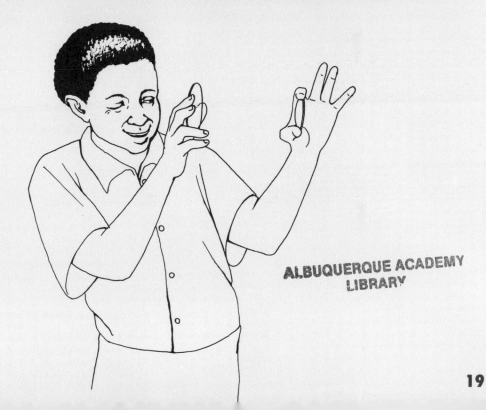

This composite photograph is made of images taken by various NASA spacecraft. The images are (from top left to top right): Jupiter, Mercury, Mars, and Saturn. Below are Venus and the Earth with its Moon in the foreground. The Sun's flare is visible behind the Earth.

TOURING THE SOLAR SYSTEM

3

Now that you've practiced some stargazing skills, it's time to find out more about what you can see by observing the night sky. Let's start with something close to home—the Moon.

OBSERVING THE MOON

The Moon is probably the most familiar sight in our nighttime sky. It shines by reflecting sunlight that falls on it. At its brightest, the Moon reflects enough light that it produces shadows here on Earth. The Moon is bright enough, in fact, that when it is overhead during the daytime you can still see it. The word **lunar** is used to describe the Moon (in Latin, *luna* means "moon").

You have probably seen the Moon often enough to have noticed that it sometimes looks like a bright, round disk, at other times like a thin crescent, and at still other times like a circle cut in half. These different shapes, which appear when the Moon is at different points in its orbit around the Earth, are called the Moon's **phases**.

When the Moon is **new**, it lies between the Earth and the Sun, so the entire half of it lit by sunshine points away from Earth. We can't see the Moon at all when it is new.

As the Moon moves a little away from the Sun, we can see a tiny sliver of its sunlit side. This very thin crescent appears in the western sky just after sunset. As the Moon orbits around Earth and continues to move east of the Sun in the sky, more and more sunlight falls on the side of the moon turned towards the Earth. The Moon is **waxing**, or growing larger.

At **first quarter** the Moon is one-quarter of the way through its orbit. When the Sun sets, the Moon is

New	First Quarter	Full	Third Quarter
		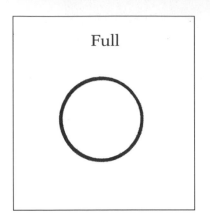	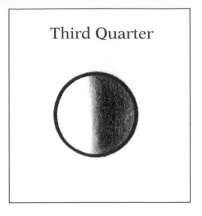

It takes the Moon 29 days to go through its phases. The cycle begins with the new Moon, which is dark. The Moon then waxes to first quarter and finally to full. Then the Moon wanes to third quarter. The visible light shrinks increasingly until the Moon is new again.

at its highest point in the sky, and we see exactly half of its sunlit side. (This is a good time to study the Moon through a telescope or binoculars. If you look along the line dividing the Moon's dark nighttime and bright daytime halves you can see the shadows of mountains on the Moon.) After first quarter, the Moon is in its **waxing gibbous** phase.

When the Moon is **full**, the side of it in sunlight faces the Earth. The Moon then lies directly opposite the Sun in our sky; as the Sun sets in the west, the full Moon rises in the east.

After the full Moon, we begin to see less and less of the Moon's sunny side. The Moon is in its **waning gibbous** phase and growing smaller. At **third quarter**, the Moon is halfway between full and new. It

looks just like the first-quarter Moon, except that it is the other half of the Moon that we see lit up.

In observing the Moon for a time, you'll probably notice that it always looks the same when it is full. This is because the Moon keeps the same face toward the Earth all the time. The Earth's gravity, acting over millions of years, has locked the Moon into this position. The Moon orbits the Earth about every 29 days, and it also spins around on its axis once every 29 days. So as the Moon orbits the Earth, it spins just enough to keep the same side always pointing toward the Earth.

As you look at the Moon you can see dark areas and light areas. The light areas, called highland areas, are the Moon's hills and mountains. The dark areas

THE MOON	
★ **EQUATORIAL DIAMETER** (*miles*)	**2,160**
★ **MASS** (*trillion trillion pounds*)	**0.16**
★ **PERIOD OF ROTATION** (*in Earth days*)	**27.3**
★ **INCLINATION OF EQUATOR** (*degrees*)	**6.5**
★ **AVERAGE ORBITAL SPEED** (*miles per hour*)	**2,112**
★ **AVERAGE DISTANCE FROM EARTH** (*miles*)	**238,000**
★ **PERIOD OF REVOLUTION** (*in Earth days*)	**29.5**

This extraordinary view of the full moon was taken by the Apollo 11 astronauts on their way back to Earth on July 21, 1969.

TRY THIS . . .

DEMONSTRATING THE MOON'S PHASES

To see for yourself why the Moon has phases, just use a ball and a table lamp. You are the Earth, the ball is the Moon, and the lamp is the Sun. With the lamp in front of you, hold the "Moon" out at arm's length from you and pivot to the left as if the Moon were orbiting about you. You will see your Moon go through a cycle of phases, just like the real Moon. (This works best if the lamp is the only light on in the room. And be careful to keep the "Moon" out of your shadow, or you won't see it in its "full" phase.) You can also do this experiment with a friend holding a flashlight as the Sun.

New Moon

First Quarter

Full Moon

Third Quarter

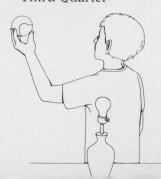

TRY THIS . . .

MAKING A MODEL OF A CRATER

You can duplicate the process of making a lunar crater by using a fine powder, such as flour, and small marbles or rocks. (Do this activity outdoors, because it can be messy!) Put a half-inch layer of flour in a shallow dish. Drop a marble into the flour and watch what happens. Try different sizes of marbles or rocks. The impact will leave a depression (the crater) and will also scatter flour. When real meteorites hit the Moon, they are moving so fast that they explode and spread debris all around the impact crater.

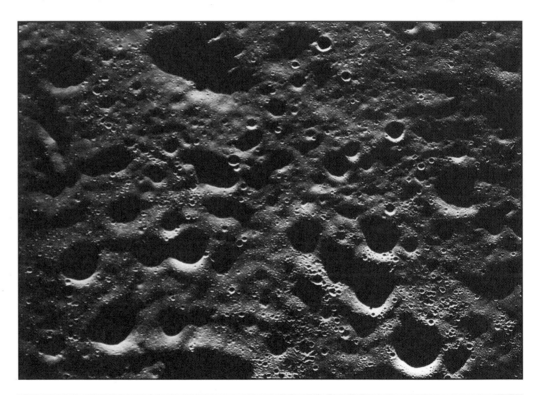

are large, fairly flat plains. Early astronomers thought these areas looked like oceans or seas so they called them **mare**, which is Latin for "sea."

The Moon is also pockmarked with countless **craters**, formed when asteroids and meteoroids strike the Moon's surface. Because the Moon has no atmosphere, small meteoroids don't burn up as they usually do on Earth but instead hit the surface at full speed,

This photo, which shows approximately 20 square miles (32 km) of lunar surface, was taken with a telephoto lens during the Apollo 8 lunar orbit mission.

from 20,000 up to 160,000 miles per hour! The meteoroid explodes when it hits the surface, and the explosion digs out a crater.

Some meteoroid explosions have been powerful enough to blast out craters nearly one hundred miles across. Scientists think that these explosions may even have knocked rocks off the Moon! As these rocks were thrown off the Moon, some were captured by the Earth's gravity and eventually crashed to the Earth as meteorites.

Many lunar craters are only a foot or so across. Many more are smaller still. Scientists found microscopic craters in the rocks brought back to Earth by the astronauts. Such tiny "zap" craters are created by space dust, which is constantly "raining" onto the Moon. Over time the rain of dust has pulverized the surface and left a powdery soil over the entire Moon.

Lunar Eclipses

The Earth casts a shadow in space, just as you do on the Earth. Earth's shadow stretches out into space. It is invisible (unless it strikes something) and is always pointed exactly opposite to the Sun. But as the Moon orbits the Earth, it sometimes passes through the Earth's shadow. This does not happen very often; since the Moon's orbit is tilted slightly, it is not usually lined up with the Sun and the Earth. When it does happen, a lunar eclipse occurs. (What phase would the Moon be in when it met the Earth's shadow?)

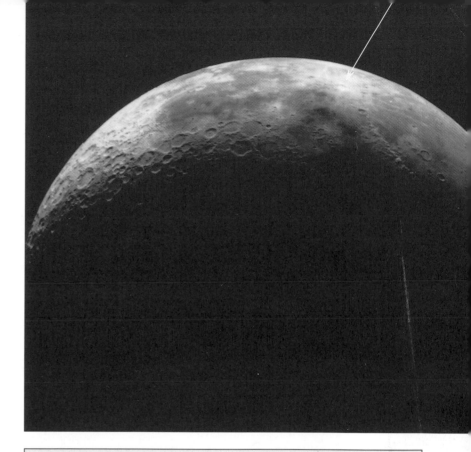

Both the dark plains of Mare Ibrium (the darker area at the top right) and the bright crater Copernicus (see arrow) are visible in this picture of the crescent Moon.

During a lunar eclipse you can see the round shadow of the Earth move across the face of the Moon and slowly darken it. However, even when the Moon is entirely within the Earth's shadow it does not disappear completely. The Moon glows with a dim red color, because red light from the Sun (the light of all Earth's sunrises and sunsets) gets bent around the Earth by the atmosphere, and enough light reaches the Moon to cause the red glow. Because the Earth's shadow is much bigger than the Moon, a lunar eclipse can last for more than an hour.

Sometimes the Moon does not pass completely into the Earth's shadow. These eclipses are called partial eclipses. During a partial eclipse the Earth's shadow darkens only a part of the Moon.

TRY THIS . . .

DEMONSTRATING WHY TWO TYPES OF LUNAR ECLIPSES OCCUR

The Earth casts two types of shadows—an *umbra* and a *penumbra*. Umbra is a Latin word meaning "shadow," and penumbra means "almost shadow." You can see what these shadows look like by performing this experiment: Shine a light onto a wall. Now put your hand in between the light and the wall. Move your hand close to the wall. Notice how your hand casts a dark shadow surrounded by a fuzzy, gray shadow. The Earth also casts a dark shadow and a fuzzy, gray shadow. The dark shadow is the umbra, and the gray shadow is the penumbra. When the Moon passes into the dark shadow, this is called an "umbral eclipse." (When it only partly enters the Earth's umbra, it is a partial eclipse.) When the Moon passes into the gray shadow, it is a "penumbral eclipse." The Moon's brightness fades so very little during a penumbral eclipse that often you wouldn't notice a penumbral eclipse even if you knew one was going on!

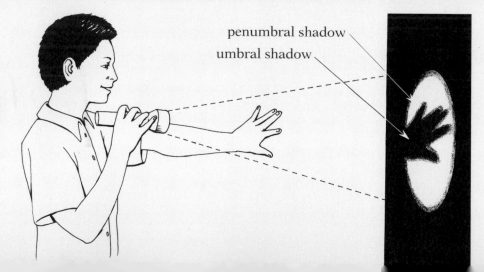

penumbral shadow
umbral shadow

DATES OF LUNAR ECLIPSES	
(VISIBLE FROM NORTH AMERICA)	
JUNE 15, 1992	Partial eclipse
DECEMBER 9, 1992	Total eclipse
JUNE 4, 1993	Total eclipse (visible from Hawaii)
NOVEMBER 29, 1993	Total eclipse
MAY 24, 1994	Partial eclipse
NOVEMBER 18, 1994	Penumbral eclipse
APRIL 15, 1995	Partial eclipse (visible from Hawaii)
APRIL 3, 1996	Total eclipse (visible on East Coast)
SEPTEMBER 27, 1996	Total eclipse

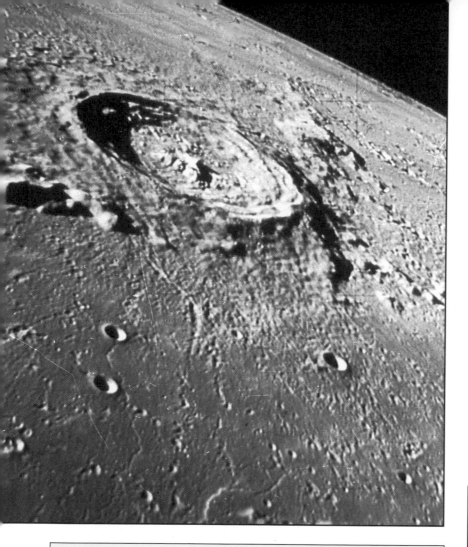

The Eratosthenes crater, the largest crater on the Moon, is a full 38 miles (60 km) across. A crater that size would have to have been made by a huge meteoroid.

OBSERVING THE SUN

IMPORTANT: NEVER LOOK DIRECTLY AT THE SUN. YOU CAN DAMAGE YOUR EYES OR BLIND YOURSELF! AND NEVER LOOK AT THE SUN THROUGH BINOCULARS OR A TELESCOPE. THESE CONCENTRATE THE SUNLIGHT AND MAKE IT EVEN MORE DANGEROUS. DO NOT LOOK AT THE SUN EVEN THROUGH TINTED GLASS OR OTHER DARK MATERIAL. THESE MAY NOT PROTECT YOUR EYES FROM THE SUN'S DAMAGING RADIATION. FOR STARGAZERS, THE SUN IS THE MOST DANGEROUS OBJECT IN THE SKY. WHEN OBSERVING THE SUN, IT IS IMPORTANT THAT YOU BE EXTREMELY CAREFUL.

The Sun is the closest star to the Earth. The Sun is of great interest to us because it is the only star close enough for us to study its surface in detail.

The Sun is a very ordinary star. It's about average in size and temperature, compared to other stars. At about 4½ billion years of age, it has lived about half its life. The Sun contains mostly hydrogen

THE SUN

★ **EQUATORIAL DIAMETER** (*miles*)	864,988
★ **MASS** (*trillion trillion pounds*)	4,385,000
★ **PERIOD OF ROTATION** (*hours*)	619
★ **INCLINATION OF EQUATOR** (*degrees*)	7

TRY THIS . . .

DEMONSTRATING THE POWER OF THE SUN

You can demonstrate the power of the Sun's light—and why it is so dangerous—by using a simple hand lens. Use the hand lens to focus sunlight on a piece of paper on the ground. (The light is focused when the dot of sunlight is perfectly round and is as small as possible.) The light may be so bright that it is hard to look at. After awhile, the paper will heat up, which you can test by touching it. It may even begin to burn. If your hand lens is powerful enough, the focused light could even start a candle wick burning!

A telescope or binoculars concentrates light just like the hand lens does, and that is why it is so dangerous to look at the Sun through a telescope. Doing this could damage your eye in an instant. SO DON'T TRY IT!

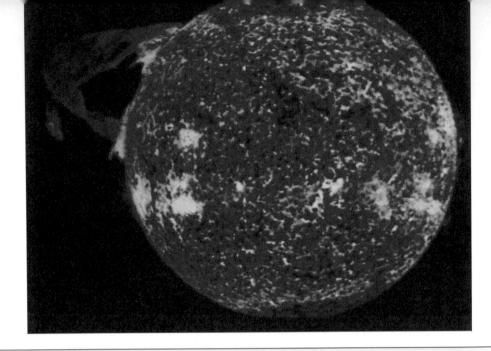

This photograph shows one of the most spectacular solar flares ever recorded, reaching more than 367,000 miles (588,000 km) out from the Sun's surface. This photo was taken on December 19, 1973, by the U.S. Naval Research Laboratory with a special camera.

and helium gas, with tiny amounts of oxygen, nitrogen, and other elements.

The Sun's energy is generated at its center, where the temperature reaches nearly 30 million degrees (compared to "only" 10,000 degrees at the surface). The Sun converts nearly 5 million tons of **matter** into energy each second in a process known as **nuclear fusion** (in which hydrogen atoms are combined, or "fused," into helium atoms). This is the same process that takes place in a "hydrogen" bomb, but the Sun can't explode like a bomb since its gravity holds it together.

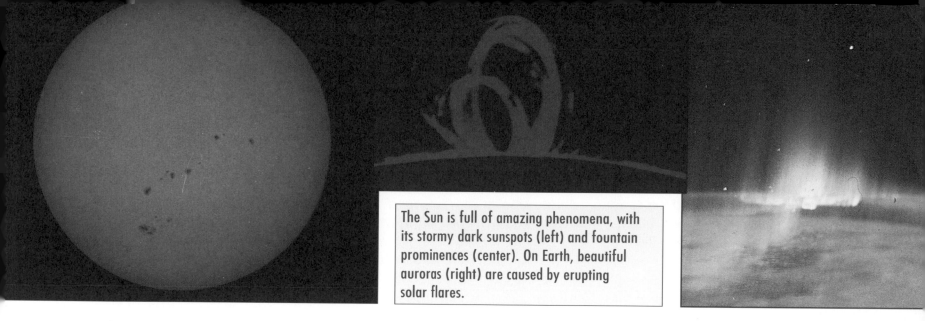

The Sun is full of amazing phenomena, with its stormy dark sunspots (left) and fountain prominences (center). On Earth, beautiful auroras (right) are caused by erupting solar flares.

Dark **sunspots** march across the fiery surface of the Sun. Sunspots are huge magnetic storms, some big enough that they could swallow the entire Earth! They appear dark because they are not as hot or bright as the rest of the Sun's surface, but they are actually a hundred times brighter than the full Moon.

Usually appearing in pairs, sunspots come and go in a cycle that lasts 11 years. They bottle up the energy of the Sun beneath them. This energy tries hard to escape, and sometimes it erupts around the sunspots in powerful **prominences** or **flares**. Prominences are clouds of hot dense gas that can rise 100,000 miles above the Sun's surface. Flares are explosions that throw out a cloud of hot gas at over a million miles per hour.

When a flare erupts, the fast-moving gas spreads out through the Solar System. When the cloud reaches the Earth, the gas particles sometimes hit the atmosphere and cause the air near the edge of space to glow, just as electricity makes a fluorescent light tube or neon sign glow. This causes beautiful **auroras**, which appear in the night sky as colorful moving curtains of light.

A powerful solar flare can also affect the Earth's magnetic field and make a compass needle point in the wrong direction. Sometimes a strong solar flare will knock out radio communications or even disrupt electrical power stations! Electric companies have had to develop special equipment to prevent damage from solar flares.

TRY THIS . . .

STUDYING SUNSPOTS

Although it is dangerous to look directly at the Sun, you can study sunspots safely by using a small telescope to project an image of the Sun onto a piece of white paper. The trick is to aim the telescope at the Sun without looking through the telescope. You can aim the telescope by watching the shadow it casts. As you move the telescope around, you will see its shadow change shape. When the shadow is as small and round as possible, the telescope is pointing straight at the Sun.

With the telescope pointing at the Sun, hold a piece of smooth, white paper about 4 to 6 inches behind the the eyepiece of the telescope. You will see the Sun's image projected on the paper. Focus the telescope until the image of the Sun is sharp. You will most likely see several black dots of various sizes on the Sun. To make sure these are really part of the Sun's image and not marks on the paper, move the paper around. If the dots stay fixed in the Sun's image, then you'll know you are looking at sunspots.

Draw an outline of the Sun's image and trace the sunspots. Do this over the next several days and keep the drawings in your observation log (tape them onto the page where you write your observing notes). You'll notice that the sunspots move across the Sun day by day. How long does it take for a spot at the center of the Sun to move to the edge? Or for a spot to move from one edge of the Sun to the other? The motion of the sunspots is caused by the Sun's rotation. By timing this motion you can figure out how long it takes the Sun to spin around one time. You'll discover that it takes about 25 days.

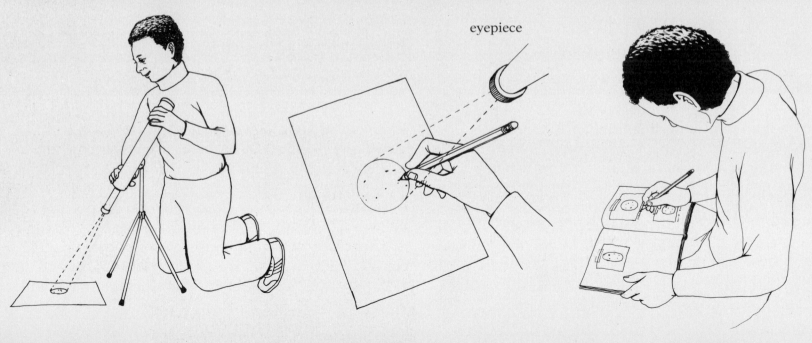

eyepiece

Solar Eclipses

Like the Earth, the Moon also casts a long shadow into space. And just as the Earth's shadow sometimes falls on the Moon, the Moon's shadow sometimes falls on the Earth. When this happens we see a solar eclipse, because the Moon has blocked the Sun from us. (What is the Moon's phase when it blocks the Sun?)

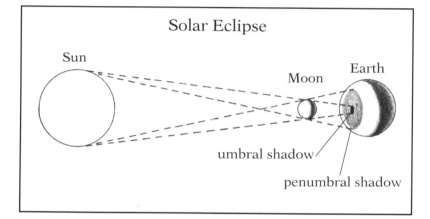

Solar Eclipse

Sun Moon Earth

umbral shadow
penumbral shadow

Viewed in Hawaii and various parts of Central America and South America, the solar eclipse of July 11, 1991, lasted an amazing 6 minutes, 53 seconds at maximum duration. ABOVE RIGHT: The corona, the outermost part of the Sun's atmosphere, is visible to the naked eye only during eclipses. RIGHT: The diamond ring effect can be seen a split second before the Moon completely covers the Sun. At that moment, a bright point of sunlight is still visible, and the Sun's corona is just beginning to be seen. FAR RIGHT: Solar prominences, too, can be seen with the naked eyes during an eclipse.

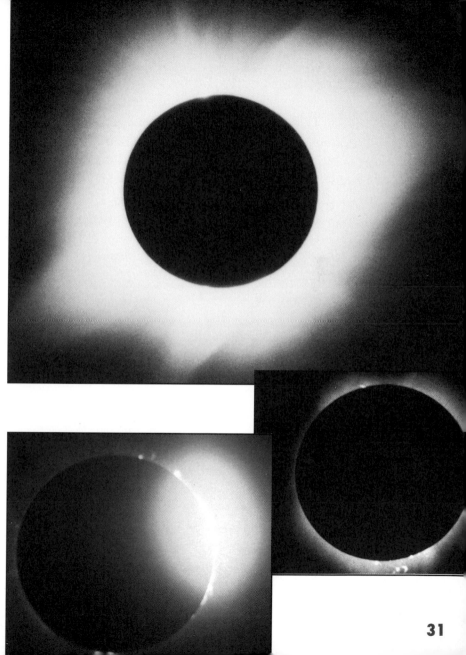

The Moon and the Sun have almost exactly the same angular size in the sky—they both appear about half a degree wide. But the Sun is about four hundred times larger than the Moon in diameter. By coincidence, it is also about 400 times farther away than the Moon, so from the Earth the Sun and Moon appear to be the same size. Every time the Sun and Moon line up just right, the Moon throws its shadow on the Earth. If the Moon's orbit were not tilted slightly, we would see a solar eclipse every month.

The Moon's shadow is only about 100 miles wide when it touches the Earth, and it moves across the Earth at a speed of more than 1,000 miles an hour. For these reasons, the total part of a solar eclipse lasts only a few minutes, though the partial phases will last up to one hour before and one hour after. To experience a total solar eclipse—when the Sun is completely blocked by the Moon—you have to be in just the right spot on the Earth. If you are not directly in the path of the Moon's shadow, you will experience

TRY THIS . . .

WATCHING A SOLAR ECLIPSE

If you're lucky enough to be in the right place at the right time to see a solar eclipse, you can watch the Moon as it covers the Sun by projecting the Sun's image—and you don't even need a telescope.

Start by making a hole about one-eighth of an inch across in a thick piece of paper or cardboard. Hold this piece of paper in the sunlight, and let the light passing through the hole fall on a white sheet of paper held a few feet away. This will project an image of the Sun that you can watch safely while the Moon moves in front of the Sun. You can make a brighter image of the Sun by making the hole in your paper bigger, but this will also make the image fuzzier. You can make a sharper image by using a smaller hole, but this will also make the image fainter. Practice projecting an image of the Sun and settling on a hole width *before* the eclipse comes!

TOTAL SOLAR ECLIPSES	
JUNE 30, 1992	South Atlantic Ocean
NOVEMBER 3, 1994	Peru, Bolivia, Paraguay, Brazil
OCTOBER 24, 1995	Iran, India, Southeast Asia
MARCH 9, 1997	Mongolia, Siberia
FEBRUARY 26, 1998	Galápagos Islands, Panama, Colombia, Venezuela, Guadeloupe, Montserrat, Antigua
AUGUST 11, 1999	Europe, Middle East, India
JUNE 21, 2001	Atlantic Ocean, Southern Africa
DECEMBER 4, 2002	Southern Africa, Indian Ocean, Australia

a partial solar eclipse (that is, you are in the Moon's penumbra, so the Moon covers only part of the Sun). Any one place on the Earth experiences a total solar eclipse only about once every 400 years.

Many people don't want to wait for a solar eclipse to come to them, so they travel to a spot on the Earth where they know the next eclipse will occur. One unlucky astronomer took 12 trips to different parts of the globe to see an eclipse, but he never saw one—every spot he visited was cloudy when the eclipse came.

OBSERVING THE PLANETS

Mercury

Mercury is the planet nearest the Sun. Mercury also moves the fastest of any planet, zipping around the Sun every 88 days (the Earth takes 365 days). Ancient Romans named the speedy planet after Mercury, the messenger of the gods.

Mercury is so close to the Sun that its surface is very hot. During the day, the temperature can climb as high as 800 degrees Fahrenheit. But because Mercury has no atmosphere to hold in the heat, at night the temperature can drop to nearly 300 degrees below zero.

Like the Moon, Mercury is covered with craters. The planet bears the scars of meteoroid collisions dating back to the early days of the Solar System.

This television photograph of Mercury was taken by the Mariner 10 spacecraft in March 1974. The largest craters seen here are about 62 miles (100 km) in diameter.

MERCURY	
⋆ **EQUATORIAL DIAMETER** (miles)	3,031
⋆ **MASS** (trillion trillion pounds)	0.729
⋆ **PERIOD OF ROTATION** (hours)	1,407.6
⋆ **INCLINATION OF EQUATOR** (degrees)	0.0
⋆ **KNOWN MOONS**	0
⋆ **AVERAGE ORBITAL SPEED** (miles per hour)	107,132
⋆ **AVERAGE DISTANCE FROM SUN** (millions of miles)	36.0
⋆ **PERIOD OF REVOLUTION** (in Earth years)	0.24

A close-up look at Mercury's craters taken by the Mariner spacecraft.

Even though Mercury is small (it's only a little bigger than the Moon), it is so near the Sun that it appears moderately bright in our nighttime sky. But because Mercury orbits so near to the Sun, it always appears close to the Sun in the sky and is difficult for us to see. The only times we can see Mercury are right after sunset (in the western sky) or right before sunrise (in the eastern sky). It will appear as a star, close to the horizon, and at best visible for only an hour.

From Earth, we lose sight of Mercury when it passes behind the Sun or between us and the Sun. Mercury is in a good position for us to observe it

TRY THIS . . .

LOOKING FOR MERCURY

Here's a list of the best dates for spotting Mercury; you can see the planet about a week before or after these dates. During these times Mercury reaches its farthest angular distance from the Sun. Watch for Mercury over several days near these dates and notice its position compared with stars near it in the sky. Sketch in your observation log the pattern of stars and Mercury's position. The changing position compared to the stars will let you know for sure that you are looking at Mercury.

DATES TO SEE MERCURY
(IN THE EASTERN SKY JUST BEFORE SUNRISE)

APRIL 23, 1992	JULY 17, 1994
AUGUST 21, 1992	NOVEMBER 6, 1994
DECEMBER 9, 1992	MARCH 1, 1995
APRIL 5, 1993	JUNE 29, 1995
AUGUST 4, 1993	OCTOBER 20, 1995
NOVEMBER 22, 1993	FEBRUARY 11, 1996
MARCH 19, 1994	JUNE 10, 1996

(IN THE WESTERN SKY JUST AFTER SUNSET)

MARCH 9, 1992	SEPTEMBER 26, 1994
JULY 6, 1992	JANUARY 19, 1995
OCTOBER 31, 1992	MAY 12, 1995
FEBRUARY 21, 1993	SEPTEMBER 9, 1995
JUNE 17, 1993	JANUARY 2, 1996
OCTOBER 14, 1993	APRIL 23, 1996
FEBRUARY 4, 1994	AUGUST 21, 1996
MAY 30, 1994	DECEMBER 15, 1996

about six times each year. But even at these favorable times, Mercury never appears more than 28 degrees away from the Sun — less than three widths of your fist at arm's length. And by the time the Sun has set and the sky near the horizon has darkened, Mercury will be much less than 28 degrees from the horizon. This makes Mercury the most difficult of the 5 naked eye planets to see.

Venus

Venus, the second planet from the Sun, is often called Earth's sister planet because the two are so similar in size. In other ways, however, they are very different. For one thing, Venus spins in the opposite direction from the Earth. And it takes 243 *days* for Venus to complete a single spin, compared to 24 hours for the Earth.

You would not want to have a picnic on Venus. It's hot enough there to melt lead! And Venus's atmosphere is about 90 times thicker than the Earth's.

VENUS

✷ **EQUATORIAL DIAMETER** (miles)	**7,521**
✷ **MASS** (trillion trillion pounds)	**10.738**
✷ **PERIOD OF ROTATION** (hours)	**5,832.2**
✷ **INCLINATION OF EQUATOR** (degrees)	**2.6**
✷ **KNOWN MOONS**	**0**
✷ **AVERAGE ORBITAL SPEED** (miles per hour)	**78,364**
✷ **AVERAGE DISTANCE FROM SUN** (millions of miles)	**67.2**
✷ **PERIOD OF REVOLUTION** (in Earth years)	**0.62**

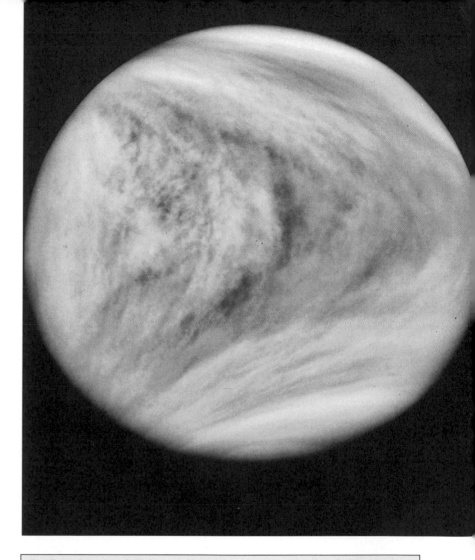

This first close-up, full-disc picture of Venus was taken by the Pioneer-Venus Orbiter spacecraft in April 1979. A turbulent, thick atmosphere wraps around the planet, and bright cloud areas cover both polar regions.

LEFT: This color-enhanced shot of Venus shows the planet's striated cloud patterns, especially at its southern pole. TOP: Scientists were able to get a look underneath Venus's hazy atmosphere with the Magellan expedition. Here, we see striking mountain ranges. ABOVE: The Sacajawea Patera Volcano, another Magellan discovery, is approximately 74 miles (120 km) wide and 133 miles (215 km) long.

If you were to stand on Venus, the pressure from the thick atmosphere would make you feel as though you were 300 feet under water!

Venus is so cloudy that we can't see its surface from the Earth. However, we have learned a lot about Venus in recent years because spacecraft from both the former Soviet Union and the United States have traveled there and sent back a great deal of information about the planet.

We know that Venus has landscapes much like those on the Earth, with rugged mountain ranges and vast, flat plains. It has large areas of land we would call "continents" if they were surrounded by oceans, but instead the surrounding basins are dry.

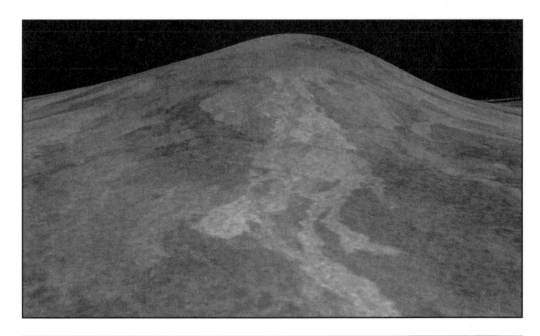

A little over one mile high, the volcano Sif Mons is more than 200 miles (320 km) in diameter.

TRY THIS . . .

CREATING A GREENHOUSE EFFECT

The runaway heating on Venus can be compared to a car parked in sunlight with the windows rolled up. The glass lets the Sun's energy enter the car, but the heat can't get out. To measure the greenhouse effect in a car on a hot day, take a thermometer and place it inside the family car. Make sure the car will be unused and parked in the sunshine for an hour or so, and roll up the car windows. Leave the thermometer in a position where you can read it without entering the car. Leave another thermometer outside the car. After an hour, compare the temperatures inside and outside the car. Even on a winter day you will find that the car becomes much hotter than the outside.

Venus also has volcanoes—some hundreds of miles wide—that once poured out rivers of lava.

Venus is about 880 degrees at its surface—even hotter than Mercury! How can Venus be hotter if Mercury is closer to the Sun? The reason is that the Venusian air is composed almost entirely of carbon dioxide, which acts like a thick blanket and creates what is called a **greenhouse effect** (that is, the gas holds in heat just like a greenhouse does). The thick atmosphere never lets Venus cool off—the Sun's energy can come in, but it can't get out.

Since Venus is farther away from the Sun than Mercury is, it can appear higher above our horizon and can be seen for a longer time in the night sky

Venus as seen it its crescent phase, in a view taken from Earth in 1964.

TRY THIS ...

LOOKING FOR VENUS

Here is a list of the best dates for spotting Venus. These are the times when Venus reaches its greatest angular distance from the Sun. You can spot Venus for several weeks before or after these dates. If you watch for Venus over several weeks near these dates, you will notice that it moves compared to the positions of the stars, just like Mercury. Make a drawing in your observation log of the stars and chart Venus's position among them. Can you see the phases of Venus through binoculars or a telescope? Draw the different phases you see in your observation log, noting the date and time of viewing.

Phases of Venus

New

Crescent

First Quarter

Full

Third Quarter

Crescent

New

DATES TO SEE VENUS
(IN THE EASTERN SKY BEFORE SUNRISE)

JUNE 10, 1993
JANUARY 13, 1995
AUGUST 19, 1996

(IN THE WESTERN SKY AFTER SUNSET)

JANUARY 19, 1993
AUGUST 25, 1994
APRIL 1, 1996

after sunset or before sunrise. In addition, Venus's cloud cover reflects a lot of sunlight, making it the brightest object in the sky apart from the Sun and the Moon. Venus is so bright that you can even see it in broad daylight, if you know where to look for it.

Venus orbits closer to the Sun than the Earth does, so it overtakes the Earth as it orbits. It circles the Sun every 224 days. Venus appears to go through phases, just like our Moon. When it passes closest to the Earth, it appears as a thin crescent. Venus is big enough that you can see its phases through a small telescope or binoculars.

Mars

Mars, the fourth planet, is farther from the Sun than the Earth is. This means Mars can shine high in the sky late at night. It doesn't have to rise or set at about the same time as the Sun, as Mercury and Venus do.

Mars shines with a reddish-orange color. The reason the planet looks red is basically that it is rusted. The Martian soil contains a lot of iron, and when iron rusts it turns red. Tiny particles of dust float in the Martian air and scatter the red light mixed up in sunlight, making the Martian sky look red.

Astronomers observing Mars through new, larger telescopes about a hundred years ago saw dark and light areas on the planet that seemed to shift and change over time. Some thought they saw sharp lines crossing the face of Mars. A few astronomers believed

MARS

★ **EQUATORIAL DIAMETER** (miles)	4,217
★ **MASS** (trillion trillion pounds)	1.416
★ **PERIOD OF ROTATION** (hours)	24.6
★ **INCLINATION OF EQUATOR** (degrees)	25.2
★ **KNOWN MOONS**	2
★ **AVERAGE ORBITAL SPEED** (miles per hour)	53,980
★ **AVERAGE DISTANCE FROM SUN** (millions of miles)	141.6
★ **PERIOD OF REVOLUTION** (in Earth years)	1.88

Like Mercury, Venus, and Earth, Mars is made of rock. This photo taken by the Viking spacecraft shows the impact craters that cover most of the Martian surface. Also visible, in the lower right, are what might be two ancient riverbeds.

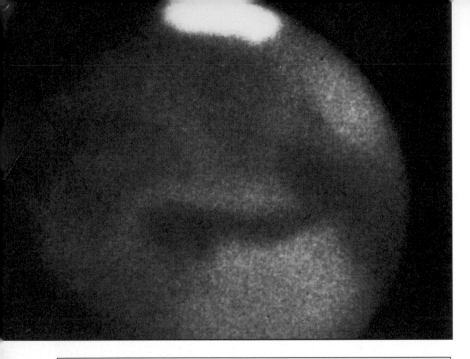

While most of the Martian surface is covered with rocks and soil, its northern pole has a huge ice cap, as shown in the photograph at left, taken through a telescope from Earth. The Viking I photograph at right was the first color photo to be taken of Mars.

that they were seeing a network of canals for carrying water. They speculated that perhaps a dying civilization of Martians had constructed a planet-wide engineering project to try to save themselves.

Today we know that there are no canals on Mars, and no other signs of civilization or life. Blurry images of Mars coupled with human imagination led some early astronomers to think they were seeing patterns and lines. However, astronomers today do believe that water once flowed on Mars since close-up pictures of the planet show ancient riverbeds and erosion caused by water.

If you could join a tour group to Mars you would see some spectacular sights. The planet has a crater from an ancient meteor impact that is about 1,000 miles wide and 4 miles deep. And Mars boasts the biggest known volcano in the solar system— Olympus Mons, which is nearly three times as high as Mount Everest and wide enough at its base to cover the entire state of Nebraska. A huge canyon on Mars might remind the tour group of Earth's Grand

Canyon—except that the Martian canyon could stretch from New York to Los Angeles and would be five times as deep.

Mars is smaller and colder than the Earth. A warm summer day on Mars might reach 60 degrees, but at night the temperature would drop to more than 100 degrees below zero. The planet has only 1/100th as much atmosphere as the Earth, which means that the surface of Mars is nearly a vacuum. In the thin atmosphere, water can exist only as ice or gas. On Earth, liquid water exists because of the pressure of our atmosphere. On Mars, liquid water bubbles away instantly, because the thin air would not press on it very much. Since we can see ancient riverbeds on Mars, there must once have been

These Martian landforms look as if they might be found on Earth. FROM LEFT, CLOCKWISE: The Olympus Mons volcano, the largest known volcano in the solar system; the Valles Marineris canyon; sand dunes in the Chryse Planitia basin.

enough atmosphere to allow liquid water to flow on the planet. The atmosphere slowly escaped into space over time. What happened to the water? Astronomers think a lot of it may now be frozen beneath the soil of Mars.

Astronomers know that the North Pole of Mars has a permanent cap of water ice. There also are caps of frozen carbon dioxide—what we call "dry ice"—at both poles. The polar caps of dry ice freeze and **sublime** with the changing Martian seasons. ("Sublime" means to change directly from a solid into a gas without ever becoming a liquid.) With a big enough telescope you can see the poles grow and shrink over time.

Mars and Earth pass closest to one another about every two years. Mars is then at its brightest and is easily visible in the nighttime sky. These times are called **oppositions** of Mars, since it is then opposite the direction of the Sun in our sky.

Through a small telescope, Mars appears as a tiny, reddish-orange disk, perhaps with a small white dot on it (the frozen ice field at the planet's pole). If the air is clear and steady enough, you might see a pattern of dark and light markings.

TRY THIS . . .

VIEWING MARS

Since Mars orbits the Sun more slowly than the Earth does, we can observe as the Earth catches and passes Mars. From Earth, Mars appears to stop, reverse direction briefly, stop, and then start moving in its original direction once more. This apparent reversal in direction, called *retrograde* motion, lasts about 10 weeks. Mars is not actually changing its motion in space. Retrograde motion is an optical illusion. It is like what you see as you pass a slower moving car on the road. For a few seconds, the slower moving car seems to move backward against more distant trees and houses.

Our ancestors puzzled over this odd motion of Mars. You can plot the motion on a star chart and see how peculiar it looks. Prepare a star chart that shows the section of the sky that Mars will be in at about the time of opposition (see table). If you plan to watch Mars through binoculars, you may wish to study this part of the sky in advance and add to your star chart any stars you can see that are not already on the chart. Two months or so before opposition, begin watching Mars and mark on your star chart where Mars appears. Do this once a week until Mars has begun its normal motion through the stars again.

DATES OF MARS OPPOSITION	
JANUARY 7, 1993	Mars in Gemini
FEBRUARY 12, 1995	Mars in Leo
MARCH 17, 1997	Mars in Virgo

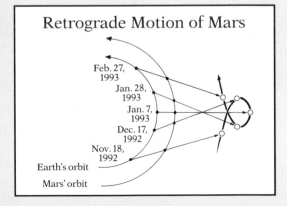

Retrograde Motion of Mars

Feb. 27, 1993
Jan. 28, 1993
Jan. 7, 1993
Dec. 17, 1992
Nov. 18, 1992
Earth's orbit
Mars' orbit

Jupiter

Jupiter, the fifth planet from the Sun, is one of the four "gas giants." It is the behemoth among the planets of the Solar System. In fact, it contains twice as much material as all the other planets combined and one thousand Earths could fit inside it. Jupiter is made mostly of hydrogen and helium (like the Sun), with other gases—such as methane and ammonia—mixed in. While Earth's atmosphere is a thin wrapping around a rocky planet, Jupiter's atmosphere is a thousand-mile-deep blanket above a vast ocean world. Earth's oceans of water are only a few miles thick, but Jupiter's oceans of hydrogen and helium make up almost the whole planet. There is no solid surface to walk on.

The weight of Jupiter's vast ocean causes the center of the planet to get very hot. This heat is released as radiation. Because of this radiated energy and because of the large number of known moons that orbit the planet (16), Jupiter is almost like a solar system in miniature.

Jupiter spins on its axis in only about 10 hours—an amazingly short time for such a huge planet! Astronomers think Jupiter's fast rotation generates its extremely strong magnetic field. This magnetic field (20,000 times stronger than the Earth's) can usually repel the solar wind, but the solar wind is sometimes strong enough to push back the field. These two forces constantly push each other back and forth.

Like all planets, Jupiter shines by reflecting sunlight (the energy Jupiter radiates is invisible). Jupiter is about 500 million miles from the Sun, yet it is so large that it reflects a lot of light. You can see Jupiter as a disk even through a small telescope or good binoculars. You will see that Jupiter is not perfectly round but looks a little "squished." This is because Jupiter's rapid spinning causes the planet to bulge around its equator. When you ride a spinning merry-go-round you feel that you are being tugged outward. This is the same type of force that makes Jupiter bulge.

JUPITER

✶ **EQUATORIAL DIAMETER** (miles)	88,730
✶ **MASS** (trillion trillion pounds)	4,187.0
✶ **PERIOD OF ROTATION** (hours)	9.8
✶ **INCLINATION OF EQUATOR** (degrees)	3.1
✶ **KNOWN MOONS**	16
✶ **AVERAGE ORBITAL SPEED** (miles per hour)	29,216
✶ **AVERAGE DISTANCE FROM SUN** (millions of miles)	483.4
✶ **PERIOD OF REVOLUTION** (in Earth years)	11.86

DATES OF JUPITER OPPOSITION

MARCH 30, 1993	Jupiter in Virgo
APRIL 30, 1994	Jupiter in Libra
JUNE 1, 1995	Jupiter in Scorpio
JULY 4, 1996	Jupiter in Sagittarius

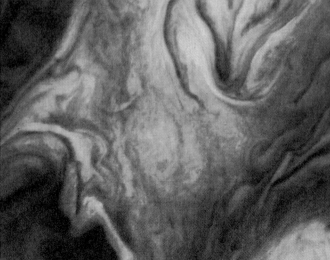

ABOVE: When it was still 29 million miles away, the Voyager spacecraft took this picture of Jupiter and two of its moons, Ganymede (right center) and Europa (top right). TOP RIGHT: A color-enhanced picture of Jupiter's violent atmosphere. RIGHT: Another close-up look at chaotic Jovian clouds.

With only a little more telescope power, you can see signs of the clouds at the top of Jupiter's atmosphere. These clouds appear as bands of color, some bluish-white and others a pale orange-red. The different colors come from the different chemicals making up the clouds; the reddish-brown clouds are chemicals like those in smog; the white clouds are mostly water ice. The clouds get stretched out into bands because of gale-force winds that roar across Jupiter.

One of the most distinctive features of Jupiter's atmosphere is the **Great Red Spot**, which peers out from the clouds like a giant red eye. Astronomers don't know for sure what causes the red color. This spot—which is big enough to swallow two Earths—is a huge storm spinning around amid the bands of clouds. The Great Red Spot has whirled through Jupiter's sky for at least three centuries since we have had telescopes good enough to see it. Although the storm seems as strong as ever, in recent years the color has faded.

Four of Jupiter's moons—**Io** (pronounced EYE-oh), **Europa**, **Ganymede**, and **Callisto**—are big enough to be seen from Earth

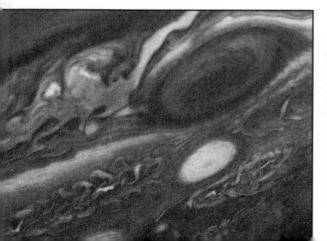

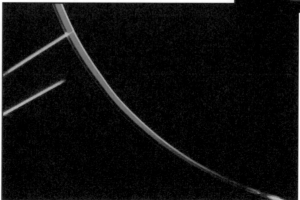

FAR LEFT: Jupiter's famous Great Red Spot, a storm more than twice as big as the Earth. LEFT: Jupiter's single ring is backlit by sunlight. ABOVE: In this composite view, Jupiter is shown with the four Galilean moons: (from top to bottom) Io, Europa, Ganymede, and Callisto.

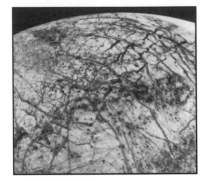

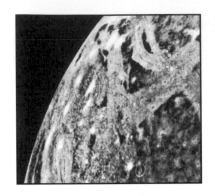

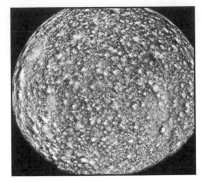

| Io with its active volcanoes. | Ice-covered Europa. | Ganymede, Jupiter's largest moon. | Callisto's heavily cratered surface. |

through binoculars or a small telescope. These moons are called the **Galilean moons**, because they were discovered in 1610 by Galileo Galilei, the first person to use a telescope. Two of the moons are as big as Mercury, and the other two are each about the size of our Moon. The rest of Jupiter's moons are much smaller. Using a small telescope, you can observe the changing positions of the Galilean moons from night to night.

The Galilean moons are very interesting places. When the Voyager spacecraft flew past Io, the Galilean moon closest to Jupiter, it photographed eight active volcanoes! These were the first active volcanoes discovered anywhere outside the Earth. (Volcanoes have since been discovered erupting on Triton, a moon of Neptune.) Io leaves a trail of sulfur particles as it orbits, creating a doughnut-shaped cloud that rings Jupiter.

The next Galilean moon farther out, Europa, seems to be made mostly of rock with a crust of frozen water. The crust is smooth, showing very few meteor crater scars. The surface of Europa must still be changing, which hides most of its craters.

Ganymede, the largest Galilean moon, probably consists of half ice and half rock. Just as on Europa, the ice lies on the outside of the moon, over a rocky core. About half of Ganymede's surface is heavily cratered by meteors. The other half doesn't show many craters but instead has long grooves, as though a giant had pulled a rake across the ice.

Callisto is the outermost of the Galilean moons. It, too, is about half ice, but instead of being smooth, its surface displays the scars of many ancient meteoroid impacts. These craters show us that Callisto's surface has not changed much in a very long time, perhaps four billion years.

TRY THIS . . .

WATCHING THE GALILEAN MOONS

You need only a pair of binoculars to follow the Galilean moons. In fact, if Ganymede, the brightest moon, were not so close to Jupiter, whose light overwhelms it, you could see it with your naked eye.

When Jupiter is in your night sky, watch it through your binoculars or telescope and draw the position of the moons in your observation log. Do this over several nights, and notice how the arrangement of the moons changes each night. You can even watch for several hours during one night and see the moons rearrange themselves. If you see all four moons on one side of Jupiter you can be reasonably sure that they are, in order outward from the planet, Io, Europa, Ganymede, and Callisto.

If you time your observation right, you may even see a moon disappear from view as it passes behind or in front of the planet. When it passes in front, you might see its shadow as a tiny dark dot on Jupiter if you have a large enough telescope and watch at high power. You might also catch sight of one of the moons as it pops back into view.

ORBITS OF THE GALILEAN MOONS ABOUT JUPITER

Io	1.8 days
Europa	3.6 days
Ganymede	7.2 days
Callisto	16.7 days

day 1 — Callisto, Io, Ganymede, Europa

day 4 — Callisto, Io, Ganymede, Europa

day 8 — Callisto, Io, Ganymede, Europa

day 12 — Callisto, Ganymede, Io, Europa

Saturn

Saturn, the sixth planet from the Sun, is also one of the gas giants. It is the second-biggest planet in the Solar System. Many people consider it to be the most beautiful, because the planet is surrounded by a mighty system of rings.

Like Jupiter, Saturn is made up of hydrogen and helium, along with other gases such as ammonia and methane. But Saturn is much colder than Jupiter. It is farther from the Sun and is too small to generate much heat on its own. It's so cold there that the ammonia is frozen. Floating through Saturn's sky like poisonous snowflakes, the ammonia forms a haze around the planet.

LEFT: Beautiful Saturn with three of its satellites: (from left to right) Rhea, Dione, and Tethys. The small black spot on Saturn's lower hemisphere is the shadow of Tethys. ABOVE: This composite view shows Saturn with 6 of its 18 known moons—Dione, Tethys, Mimas, Enceladus, Rhea, and Titan.

The Voyager spacecraft took many photographs of Saturn's rings. ABOVE: The rings' shadows are cast on the planet's surface (Tethys and Dione are in the foreground). CENTER AND ABOVE RIGHT: Two more views of the rings, one color enhanced and the other showing the rings as they actually appear. RIGHT: Saturn's largest moon, Titan, has a thick, hazy atmosphere.

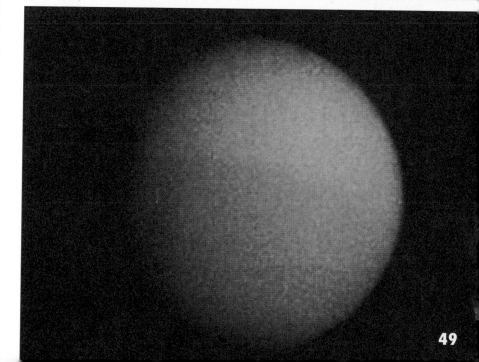

SATURN

★ **EQUATORIAL DIAMETER** *(miles)*	**74,600**
★ **MASS** *(trillion trillion pounds)*	**1,253.8**
★ **PERIOD OF ROTATION** *(hours)*	**10.2**
★ **INCLINATION OF EQUATOR** *(degrees)*	**26.7**
★ **KNOWN MOONS**	**17**
★ **AVERAGE ORBITAL SPEED** *(miles per hour)*	**21,565**
★ **AVERAGE DISTANCE FROM SUN** *(millions of miles)*	**886.7**
★ **PERIOD OF REVOLUTION** *(in Earth years)*	**29.46**

TRY THIS . . .

OBSERVING SATURN AND ITS RINGS

You will need to use a telescope in order to be able to distinguish the rings of Saturn from the planet itself. At certain times you may even be able to see the shadow of the rings on the planet. Under good conditions, you can also catch sight of the Cassini Division, a dark band near the outside of the rings.

The brightness of Saturn varies considerably, depending on the orientation of its rings. When the rings are tipped toward us so they appear at their widest, the rings are brighter than the planet itself. The rings will not be in this position for us until 2003 (the last time was in 1988).

You can observe Saturn's rings "disappearing" when Earth and Saturn line up in such a way that we are looking exactly along the plane of the rings.

DATES OF SATURN OPPOSITION

AUGUST 19, 1993	Saturn in Capricorn
SEPTEMBER 1, 1994	Saturn in Aquarius
SEPTEMBER 14, 1995	Saturn in Pisces
SEPTEMBER 26, 1996	Saturn in Pisces

DATES WHEN RINGS "DISAPPEAR"

MAY 21, 1995
AUGUST 11, 1995
FEBRUARY 11, 1996

Saturn has bands of clouds similar to those on Jupiter, except that the colors of the bands on Saturn are not very distinct. The bands are difficult to see from the Earth, and even close-up views sent back by spacecraft do not show much detail in the clouds. However, Voyager did spot a storm system similar to Jupiter's Great Red Spot, but it is not as big or as colorful.

Compared to many of the stars in the sky, Saturn is not very bright. Finding it will be easier if you memorize its location among the constellations by consulting a star chart. It takes Saturn nearly 30 years to orbit the Sun, so it moves slowly against the background of stars. To the naked eye, Saturn appears as a yellowish star. When you look at the planet through a small telescope, though, its appearance is unmistakable because of its distinctive rings.

Saturn's rings contain an uncountable number of little moons that are spread in a thin band around the middle of the planet. Some of the particles in the rings are as tiny as snowflakes, while others are as big as houses. Astronomers think the ring particles are made mostly of frozen water. Nobody is really sure where the particles came from, but most likely a large, icy body came so close to Saturn that it was torn apart by the planet's gravity. Or, the rings may be the debris left from the collision of a comet with one of Saturn's moons.

Astronomers think the rings may be only 100 feet or so thick. But they spread more than 250,000 miles wide — about the distance from the Earth to the Moon! The rings are actually made of many individual ringlets, which are narrow ribbons of icy particles. There are gaps between some sections of ringlets. The largest gap, named the **Cassini Division** after the astronomer who, in 1675, first spotted it, can be seen through a small telescope.

Dione

Tethys

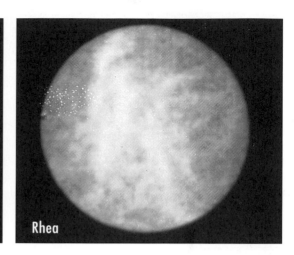

Rhea

Because Saturn is tilted a bit, we see different amounts of the rings at different times. Sometimes the planet is aligned so the rings are tipped toward us and appear very bright. At other times the rings are edge-on to us and are so thin that they virtually disappear from sight.

Saturn has 18 moons that we know of. One of them, **Titan**, is big enough to be seen easily from Earth through a small telescope or binoculars. Through a telescope, Titan may look like a star near Saturn. If you watch it from one night to the next, however, you'll be able to see it change positions on its 16-day orbit around the planet. Dione, Tethys, and Rhea are smaller, slightly fainter, moons you may also see with a small telescope.

Titan is bigger than the planet Mercury and has a cloudy atmosphere that contains a great deal of nitrogen gas (so does the Earth's atmosphere). It is so far from the Sun that Titan's temperature is about 220 degrees below zero (F) and some of its cloud-covered mountains may be made of ice.

Uranus, Neptune, and Pluto

Besides Jupiter and Saturn, the other two gas giants are Uranus and Neptune, the seventh and eighth planets from the Sun. Though they are not nearly as big as the first two, Uranus and Neptune are still much larger than the Earth. Right now, Neptune enjoys the reputation of being the farthest planet from the Sun. Pluto, usually the ninth planet from the Sun, is a small, frozen ball that has a very elliptical orbit that sometimes brings it closer to the Sun than Neptune. This is now the case, and will be so until 1999.

Uranus, Neptune, and Pluto are so distant from us that they were not discovered until after the telescope was invented. Uranus was discovered in 1781 by an astronomer named William Herschel, who worked with a homemade six-inch telescope. Observing the stars one night, he noticed a "fuzzy" shape that he knew was not a star. He watched it over several more weeks until he could figure out its orbit. He realized he had found a new planet, one unknown to the millions of stargazers who had lived before him.

Uranus can actually be seen with the naked eye, when conditions are very good and if you know exactly where to look for it. Uranus shines with a pale greenish-blue color, but it is so faint that it is easily overlooked. If you try to spot Uranus, its color may help you to distinguish it from the stars.

Neptune was discovered in 1846. In this case, astronomers had actually been looking for it! Two astronomers—John Adams and Urbain Leverrier, who worked independently of each other—had studied Uranus and noticed that it did not move smoothly. They calculated that the gravity of another, more distant planet must be tugging on Uranus and disturbing its orbit. The two predicted where this next planet should be, and when other astronomers aimed their telescopes to this part of the sky they found Neptune. Neptune is too faint to be seen with the naked eye, but with care you can spot it using binoculars or a telescope.

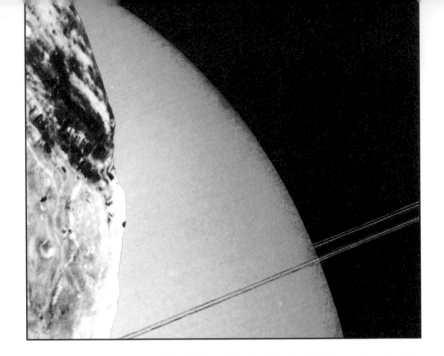

A superimposed image shows greenish-blue Uranus behind its satellite, Miranda.

URANUS

* ★ **EQUATORIAL DIAMETER** *(miles)*..............................**31,600**
* ★ **MASS** *(trillion trillion pounds)*.......................................**190.95**
* ★ **PERIOD OF ROTATION** *(hours)*..................................**17.2**
* ★ **INCLINATION OF EQUATOR** *(degrees)*............................**82.1**
* ★ **KNOWN MOONS**...**15**
* ★ **AVERAGE ORBITAL SPEED** *(miles per hour)*.................**15,234**
* ★ **AVERAGE DISTANCE FROM SUN** *(millions of miles)*...**1,784.0**
* ★ **PERIOD OF REVOLUTION** *(in Earth years)*......................**84.01**

NEPTUNE

* **EQUATORIAL DIAMETER** (miles)................................**30,700**
* **MASS** (trillion trillion pounds)...................................**226.0**
* **PERIOD OF ROTATION** (hours)..............................**16.1**
* **INCLINATION OF EQUATOR** (degrees)....................**29.0**
* **KNOWN MOONS**..**8**
* **AVERAGE ORBITAL SPEED** (miles per hour)..................**12,147**
* **AVERAGE DISTANCE FROM SUN** (millions of miles)....**2,794.4**
* **PERIOD OF REVOLUTION** (in Earth years)......................**164.79**

Like Jupiter, Neptune has its own giant storm system. Called the Great Dark Spot, it is about the size of one Earth. BELOW: A close-up look at cloud streaks high in Neptune's atmosphere.

Neptune and Uranus are both so far away that they appear very tiny, even through a large telescope. Through a small one, they won't look much different from stars, and because their orbits are so large they move very slowly against the background of stars. You will need to use a star chart and become familiar with the stars around Uranus and Neptune before you'll be able to spot these distant planets.

Pluto was not discovered until 1930. The planet is so small and so far away that only very large telescopes are strong enough to spot it.

PLUTO

★ **EQUATORIAL DIAMETER** *(miles)*	1,420
★ **MASS** *(trillion trillion pounds)*	0.026
★ **PERIOD OF ROTATION** *(hours)*	6.4
★ **INCLINATION OF EQUATOR** *(degrees)*	62.0
★ **KNOWN MOONS**	1
★ **AVERAGE ORBITAL SPEED** *(miles per hour)*	10,604
★ **AVERAGE DISTANCE FROM SUN** *(millions of miles)*	3,656.0
★ **PERIOD OF REVOLUTION** *(in Earth years)*	247.70

OBSERVING OTHER SOLAR SYSTEM OBJECTS

Asteroids

Asteroids may be the pieces of a planet that never came together when the Solar System was forming. Astronomers estimate that there may be as many as a million asteroids, the exact number depending on how small a piece of rock you care to count as an asteroid. Over 4,000 asteroids have been discovered in the past 150 years, and we now find about two dozen new ones each year.

Since asteroids are all fairly small—the largest only six hundred miles across—and usually far away, they appear only as points of light even through binoculars or a telescope. The only way to distinguish them from stars is by their movement, which you would have to plot on a star chart over several nights to notice.

TRY THIS . . .

OBSERVING METEOR SHOWERS

Well-known meteor showers occur on the dates shown. Plan to go to a dark spot, dress warmly, get comfortable, and look up. You will see more meteors after midnight, but you'll see enough in the early night to make the observing worthwhile. Since most meteors are very faint, the best viewing occurs when the Moon is not out, so that the sky is as dark as possible. As your eyes adapt to the dark you'll be able to see not only bright meteors but many faint ones as well. If you watch long enough, you will notice that the meteors in a shower seem to come from the same area of the sky. The showers are named after the constellation nearest this part of the sky.

Note in your observation log how many meteors you see. Trace their paths on a star chart. Notice how their paths all seem to point to the same place.

The number of meteors we can see in a shower varies greatly from year to year. For example, one night in 1966 the Leonids lit up the sky with 2,000 visible meteors each minute for a short time!

RECURRING METEOR SHOWERS

NAMES	DATES	NUMBER OF METEORS PER HOUR (VARIES)
Quadrantids	JANUARY 1–4	40
Lyrids	APRIL 20–22	15
Eta Aquarids	MAY 3–5	20
Delta Aquarids	JULY 26–30	20
Perseids	AUGUST 9–15	50
Orionids	OCTOBER 20–24	25
Leonids	NOVEMBER 14–20	10
Geminids	DECEMBER 10–13	60

The Leonid Fireball (an unusually bright meteor) was seen during the Leonids meteor shower on November 17, 1966.

Meteor Showers

Meteor showers are great fun to watch. The sight of a bright meteor streaking silently across the sky is thrilling, and during a meteor shower you can marvel at a great many of these cosmic "fireworks."

Millions of small meteoroids about the size of sand grains rain down on the Earth from space constantly. In fact, at least 100 tons of this debris falls into the Earth's atmosphere each day!

Most meteoroids burn up through friction as they pass through the Earth's upper atmosphere at very high speed. On a clear, dark night we can see about three meteors each hour in the early evening and six each hour between midnight and dawn.

Several times each year the Earth passes through streams of space debris that orbit the Sun, the remnants of old comets. During these times we are treated to the spectacular sight of a meteor shower.

Meteorites weighing several tons have been recovered after they hit the Earth's surface, though most are much smaller. There are also many micrometeorites no bigger than pieces of dust. If you run your finger over any dusty surface, some of the dust you pick up is space dust! It could even be as old as the Solar System—about 4.5 billion years old.

Comets

A comet can be a magnificent sight in the nighttime sky. But more often a comet is a faint, easily overlooked celestial event.

Comets are, basically, dirty snowballs. They are mixtures of frozen water and gases mixed with dust and other solid particles. Astronomers think comets

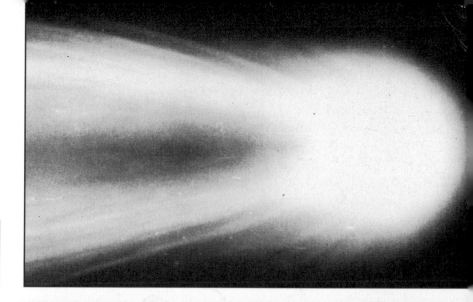

BELOW: This photo of Halley's comet was taken when the comet passed close to the Earth in 1986. RIGHT: A close-up of the head on Halley's Comet, taken in 1910.

are frozen remainders from the cloud of material that formed the Solar System billions of years ago, so they study comets to learn what that original material was like.

Comets usually orbit the Sun far beyond the planets, but occasionally one falls inward toward the Sun. Some comets fall into the Sun or pass so close to it that they are destroyed. Others fall past the Sun once, then skip out of the Solar System forever. And some, such as Halley's comet, settle into new orbits and pass close to the Sun at regular intervals. Halley's comet passed close to the Sun in 1910 and 1986 and is due back for another passage in 2062.

When a comet comes near the Sun, the sunlight causes the frozen gases to sublime, or change directly from a solid into a gas. As the gases are released, the solar wind pushes them out into a faint, glowing tail. The solid particles are also released, and the pressure of sunlight pushes them away from the comet to form another tail made of dust. To see a comet in its full glory, you need to look for it just after sunset in the western sky or just before sunrise in the eastern sky.

TRY THIS . . .

COLLECTING METEORITES AND MICROMETEORITES

There are several ways to collect micrometeorites. Next time you go to the beach or a lake, take a magnet with you and use it to sift through the sand. Of the particles that collect on the magnet, up to 10 percent may be micrometeorites. You can also collect rain water or snow in a pail. Run your magnet through the water or melted snow and see how many particles your magnet collects. Again, many of these particles will be micrometeorites. If you have access to a microscope, you can study these particles through it.

Bigger meteorites are much rarer and harder to find unless they land in a special location. For example, scientists in Antarctica have discovered that meteorites can be found on the ice fields there. Since the native rocks are covered by a thick sheet of ice, the scientists know that any rock on top of the ice must have fallen from outer space.

Most of us can't go to Antarctica, but we can go to other places where there are usually no native rocks on the surface—for example, the dried lake beds of the southwestern United States—and look for rocks that are likely to be meteorites.

TRY THIS . . .

MAKING A COMET

You can make a miniature comet and watch as it sublimates—just like a real comet being heated by the Sun! Make sure you ask for an adult's help with this activity.

The materials you will need are dry ice (frozen carbon dioxide), a large bowl or pot, a plastic garbage bag, several smaller plastic bags, rubber gloves, a hammer, water, sand or dirt, and a few drops of ammonia.

You can buy dry ice (you'll need about two cups) from a company that sells ice or from some ice cream stores. *Be very careful in handling dry ice, and always wear rubber gloves. Frozen carbon dioxide is much colder than frozen water, and if it touches your skin it will hurt as if you had been burned by fire.*

Use a plastic garbage bag to line a bowl or pot big enough to hold at least a quart. Put two cups of water into the lined bowl. Add a couple of spoonfuls of sand. Sprinkle in a few drops of ammonia, and stir the mixture well.

Wearing your gloves, wrap the chunk of dry ice in several plastic bags. Use a hammer or rock to pound the dry ice and break it into many small pieces. When the dry ice is crushed, add about two cups of it while stirring your comet "soup." Keep stirring while the dry ice freezes the water. When the mixture is almost completely frozen, lift it up using the plastic liner of your bowl and shape the wrapped mixture into a ball. When the "comet" is frozen and can hold its shape on its own, unwrap it and set it somewhere you can watch it.

The dry ice will sublimate into a gas. You may see jets of carbon dioxide shoot from your comet. After a while, your comet will shrink and become pitted, like a comet that has been eroded by the Sun.

(BASED ON A RECIPE BY DENNIS SCHATZ, PACIFIC SCIENCE CENTER, SEATTLE, WASHINGTON)

Satellites

While you are outside watching the stars, you may occasionally see a starlike dot of light moving slowly and steadily across the sky. You have spotted an artificial satellite, a human-made object orbiting the Earth (the Moon, in contrast, is a natural satellite). Some satellites relay telephone calls or television reports, others study the Earth or space for scientists. A few, like the "Mir" space station, built by the former Soviet Union, carry people. The U.S. Space Shuttle is a satellite too, while it's in space! Other satellites are junk, such as broken satellites or parts of rockets that were used to lift satellites into orbit. Right now there are thousands of these artificial satellites orbiting the Earth. A satellite in a near-Earth orbit just a few hundred miles up moves at more than 16,000 miles per hour and takes about an hour and a half to complete one orbit.

Sometimes as a satellite crosses the sky, it will suddenly disappear! What has happened? Satellites shine only by reflecting sunlight and this one has passed into the shadow of the Earth. Thus, we can observe that the Earth's shadow does indeed stretch into space, even the nearby space in which satellites travel.

FURTHER EXPLORING

You've done your first exploration of our big backyard — the Solar System. The more time you spend under the night sky visiting and revisiting these sights, the more familiar they will become to you and the easier they will be for you to find.

In many areas, amateur astronomers have regular meeting times when they set up their telescopes. Most amateur astronomers gladly welcome other people to share the view through their telescopes. You can contact an amateur astronomy group to find out when and where they set up telescopes for stargazing. Ask your local library or college if there's an amateur astronomy club in your area.

Science centers and planetariums also often have telescopes and schedule regular viewing nights for stargazers. A planetarium also is a good place to become familiar with the motions of the stars and planets and to help you learn the various constellations.

There are several magazines for stargazers — for example, *Odyssey* (for children) and *Astronomy* and *Sky & Telescope*. You can probably find them at your library or at a magazine store, or you can subscribe to them. You can also order sets of sky charts for each month that show when and where planets and other objects can be found. You can subscribe to these charts for $6 a year from Abrams Planetarium, Michigan State University, East Lansing, MI 48824.

So far, you have explored only a tiny section of the universe. But there is much, much more available to a dedicated stargazer. There are many more exciting things to see in the night sky, and a lifetime in which to get to know the cosmic community in which we live.

angular distance The apparent size of an object or the apparent distance between two objects as measured in degrees.

asteroid A small, rocky, or metal object that orbits the sun like a miniature planet. Most asteroids are found between Mars and Jupiter; Ceres, the biggest asteroid known, is 600 miles wide, but most asteroids are only a couple of miles across.

aurora The glow produced by gases in the Earth's atmosphere when they become charged by energy from the Sun.

Callisto One of the four Galilean moons orbiting Jupiter.

Cassini Division A broad, dark gap in the rings of Saturn; it can be seen from the Earth through a telescope.

comet A ball of frozen gases, ice, dust, and small rock particles that forms a long, glowing tail when it nears the Sun.

constellation A pattern of stars in the night sky.

crater The hole created when a meteorite hits a planet or moon.

degrees A unit for measuring angles; there are 360 degrees in a circle.

Earth Third planet from the Sun; our home world.

Europa One of the four Galilean moons orbiting Jupiter.

eyepiece A small lens that projects the image made by a telescope or binoculars into the eye and magnifies that image.

first-quarter Moon Phase of the Moon when it is one-quarter of the way through its cycle; the half-circle shape of the first-quarter Moon can be seen high overhead at sunset.

flare An explosion on the Sun that sends clouds of hot, charged gas out through the Solar System. Flares can cause bright auroras and disrupt radio communications on Earth.

focus The effect of a curved lens or mirror to concentrate a beam of light into a small, sharp image. The point at which such an image is formed.

full Moon Phase of the Moon when its sunlit side points directly toward Earth; the full Moon is opposite the Sun in the sky.

Galilean moons The four biggest moons orbiting Jupiter; first seen by Galileo nearly 400 years ago.

Ganymede One of the four Galilean moons orbiting Jupiter.

gas giants The four largest planets in the Solar System; these consist mostly of hydrogen and helium and have thick atmospheres.

gibbous The point in the Moon's cycle where more than half but not all of the Moon is illuminated.

Great Red Spot A storm more than twice the size of the Earth that has raged on Jupiter for more than 300 years.

greenhouse effect Heating caused when energy from the Sun is trapped by gases in a planet's atmosphere.

horizon The line where the body of the Earth cuts off the sky from view.

image A representation of an object made by a lens or mirror.

Io One of the four Galilean moons orbiting Jupiter.

Jupiter Fifth planet from the Sun; the first of the gas giants and the biggest object in the Solar System after the Sun.

lens A piece of glass shaped so that light passing through it is redirected to form a concentrated image.

lunar Used to describe the Moon; *luna* means "moon" in Latin.

lunar eclipse When the full Moon moves through Earth's shadow and is darkened partially or totally.

mare A flat, dark area on the Moon, named after the Latin word for "sea."

Mars Fourth planet from the Sun and the first one beyond Earth's orbit.

matter The stuff of which the universe is made: solids, liquids, gases, or isolated atoms or particles.

Mercury The closest planet to the Sun.

meteor A streak of light caused when a small piece of rock (a meteoroid) from space enters the Earth's atmosphere.

meteorite The remnant of a meteoroid that has not completely burned up in the atmosphere and has reached Earth's surface.

meteoroid A small piece of rock or metal found in space between the planets; meteoroids are typically the size of a piece of dust, but can be as big as a house or bigger.

meteor shower The appearance of many meteors in the night sky as the Earth crosses the orbit of a meteoroid stream.

Moon The Earth's natural satellite. The natural satellites orbiting many of the other planets in the Solar System are also called moons.

naked eye Stargazing using only your eyes, without the aid of a telescope or binoculars.

Neptune The farthest gas giant and the most distant planet from the Sun until the year 1999.

new Moon Phase of the Moon when it is between the Earth and the Sun.

northern lights The aurora seen in the Northern Hemisphere.

nuclear fusion The process by which lightweight atoms are combined into heavier atoms and energy is released. Nuclear fusion provides the energy needed for the Sun and other stars to shine.

objective The light-gathering lens or mirror in a telescope.

opposition The position in which a planet and the Sun are in opposite parts of the sky, as seen from the Earth.

penumbra The partial shadow of an object (such as a planet or moon); some of the Sun's light appears in this shadow.

phases The different appearances of the Moon as it orbits the Earth. Venus also shows phases as it orbits the Sun.

planet One of nine large bodies in our Solar System that orbit the Sun.

planetarium A theater that re-creates the appearance of the night sky by projecting images of the stars and planets on a curved screen.

planisphere A star chart that can be adjusted to show what heavenly bodies are in the sky at any time of the year.

Pluto A small, frozen world that is usually the most distant planet from the Sun.

prominence A fountain or loop of hot gas that rises above the Sun's surface.

reflector A telescope that uses a mirror as its objective.

refractor A telescope that uses a lens as its objective.

retrograde The apparent temporary westward motion of a planet among the stars.

satellite A small body in orbit about a larger body in space; natural satellites are often called moons.

Saturn One of the gas giants and the sixth planet from the Sun; famous for its bright rings.

sol The Latin name for the Sun.

solar eclipse A time when the Moon blocks the Sun from view.

Solar System The Sun and all its planets, moons, meteors, comets, and asteroids.

solar wind An outflow of gas particles from the Sun.

southern lights The aurora seen in the Southern Hemisphere.

star chart A "road map" of the sky, showing the positions of the visible stars.

sublime To change directly from a frozen solid to a gas without becoming a liquid.

Sun The star that sits at the center of the Solar System.

sunspots Magnetic storms on the Sun that appear as dark spots.

third-quarter Moon Phase of the Moon three-quarters of the way through its cycle; the half circle shape of the third-quarter Moon can be seen high overhead at sunrise.

Titan The largest of Saturn's moons, and the only moon in the Solar System with a thick atmosphere.

umbra The darkest shadow cast by an object.

universe The collection of all the matter and energy that we know about or can learn of through science.

Uranus The seventh plant from the Sun and one of the four gas giants.

Venus The second planet from the Sun; has a dense, cloudy atmosphere and the hottest surface in the Solar System except for the Sun.

waning Becoming smaller; used to describe the Moon as it moves from its full to its new phase and its sunlit side slowly disappears from view.

waxing Growing larger; used to describe the Moon as it moves from its new to its full phase and increasing amounts of its sunlit side come into view.

zenith The point in the sky directly overhead.